# Faith Without Borders

*A devotional to inspire you to step out in faith*

**Virginia Martin**

# DEDICATION

God – my Father, Mentor, and Savior. To Him be all the glory always.

Cristina Isabel Diaz – my firstborn, best friend, confidant, and greatest supporter in everything. Thank you for being by my side through it all. Never lose the child in you.

Samantha Anne Rivera – my youngest, spirited, dedicated and determined. Your smile lights up a room. I am proud of the woman you have become and are yet to be.

Noemi Gonzalez – my God sent Angel. Thank you for being an obedient child of God and saving me from myself.

The Lighthouse Church – my church and inspiration in writing this devotional. Part of the proceeds from the sale of this book will benefit their ministry and future City Center project.

*"For I am not seeking my own good but the good of many, so that they may be saved. Follow my example, as I follow the example of Christ."*

*– 1 Corinthians 10:33, 11:1*

# ACKNOWLEDGMENTS

God - for the motivation and guidance in writing this book.

B.J. Tiernan – author and friend –  Thank you for keeping the writing spark alive in me through your teachings, and not allowing me to give up my dream of being a writer.

Thank you to my family and friends who have supported me throughout my trials and triumphs. You know who you are.

VIRGINIA MARTIN

*"But the Lord stood at my side, and gave me strength, so that through me the message might be fully proclaimed..."*

*– 2 Timothy 4:17*

# TABLE OF CONTENTS

# CONGRATULATIONS!!!

Dear Karen,

Thank you for entering the Faith Without Borders Goodreads giveaway.

You have won a signed paperback version of my book.

I hope you enjoy the read. :)

# INTRODUCTION

*"My soul finds rest in God alone; my salvation comes from him. He alone is my rock and my salvation; he is my fortress, I will never be shaken." – Psalm 62:1-2*

Are you feeling despair, confusion or loneliness? Is your life not making sense, and you don't know which way to turn or how to deal with your trials and tribulations? You are not alone, God is here to comfort, heal and shine his light on you.

In *Faith Without Borders* I share my testimony, and the good news of God's grace. You can and will pull through, by trusting God, and letting him be your strength in times of weakness. I learned that as long as I am with God, I am all right.

My life changed, and I was transformed, when I accepted Jesus Christ as my Lord and Savior. I shout out to the world that God restores the weary and uplifts the spirit of the broken hearted. You will not be the same once you read *Faith Without Borders*. Let the readings in each chapter sink into your soul. God's message is clear, simple and full of hope. Get ready to receive his blessing.

*Come unto me all that are faithful, and obedient. Those that follow me will reap the rewards of eternal life. While on Earth, you will be blessed by my grace. Follow my will for you, trust in my timing, keep hope alive and believe in me always.*

# POINTS FOR REFLECTION

Enhance your life: Experience and know God through prayer and reading the Bible.

Find hope through faith in God:  It is about you and God, have a personal connection and relationship with him.

God loves you and is with you always:  Let him rescue and restore you.

God  knows where to lead you and clear the muddled waters in your path: Let him in all areas of your life.

Let God be alive and well in you:  Accept Jesus Christ as your Lord and Savior and your life will be transformed.

Learn to leave things you can't control in God's hands: Remember that it is his will be done, not yours.  This makes all the difference.

Look for God in all the right places, and you won't ever be lost again.

God has already been in your tomorrow, and is working on your today.

VIRGINIA MARTIN

*"My heart is stirred by a noble theme as I recite my verses for the king; my tongue is the pen of a skillful writer."*

*– Psalm 45:10*

# 1 CHOICES

*"He reached down from on high and took hold of me; he drew me out of deep waters." – Psalm 18:16*

God gives us freedom of choice. We either choose him and his way or another way. Though this sounds simple enough, it is not, especially if you do not know who God really is, and have no clue about his way. I lived my life blindly, trusting myself, family or friends to help me decide on something important, or tell me what step to take next. I never thought to ask God for the choice(s) I should make in many areas of my life, which led to confusion and second guessing my decisions.

I could probably list a few bad decisions I made in my life. Some examples are: getting married too young, not going to a four year college after high school, not going back to my mother's hospital room to say goodbye to her, when I realized she was not going to make it, because I didn't want to come to terms with that reality, and not keeping up with close friends and family when I moved to Florida. These choices made me live with regret. Having God in my life at these times would have made a difference in the outcome.

Even though I did not "talk" to God, I still got a "pit in my stomach" feeling when I was not sure about doing something. I ignored my instincts, which I realize now was God's way of talking to me. He loved me even when I had not yet accepted him or Jesus Christ into my heart. With God there is a clear, straight and narrow path you walk, because he leads you, and there is no doubt of the direction you are going. It has taken me a while, but I pray to him for every choice I have to make, especially if it will have a major impact in my life, and I won't have it any other way. When you have doubt about anything, then it is time to pray, and wait on what God has to say. You will be glad you did, since there is no need to pay any consequence if God is behind your decision.

Several years ago, I made a choice that changed my life forever. I married someone that I thought was God sent, and a second chance at love. The man knew God and quoted Scripture, and told me God had a purpose for him. I uprooted and relocated out of state to where he lived to start a new life. However, shortly after I moved there, my world started caving in, as I became a victim of mental, emotional and verbal abuse. The man that professed to love me did not practice what he preached. He had demons of his own that he had not dealt with.

Through my trials in this marriage I learned a few things that served as life lessons: you cannot "fix" someone that does not want to be fixed, mold yourself to their liking, or turn into someone you are not, just to keep them happy. God must also be in the center of any relationship. Furthermore, I didn't love myself enough to know that I did not deserve to be mistreated. I lost the person I was, and fell into a state of despair.

*"Many are the plans in a man's heart, but it is the Lord's purpose that prevails." – Proverbs 19:21*

But, God heard my cries and sent an angel in human form to save me. She obeyed God by coming to where I was, though she did not understand why. Her plans were to go somewhere else on her vacation, not her brother's house. Yet, it all made sense when she saw how distraught I was. I would not be here today if it were not for her intervention. Her advice to me was to read the Bible every day, in order to get to know God, and help find answers that would help me decide what to do with my life, and the situation I was living in. However, in order for me to hear God's word, I needed to have an open mind, heart and total faith in God. She said I mattered to him and not to give up. I gave my life to God and accepted Jesus Christ, as my

Lord and Savior, in May, 2009, and this was the best choice I have ever made. I gave God full access to my life. Needless to say, my marriage ended, and I returned home and never looked back. I had to build myself up again and God was there for that too.

*"Therefore, if anyone is in Christ, he is a new creation; the old has gone, the new has come!"- 2 Corinthians 5:17*

I started my spiritual journey, and it is a process not to be rushed. It has taken time for me to heal, but I have. God forgave me my wrong choice in partner, so who was I not to pay it forward and forgive too. I no longer let anyone control me, only God does that. I share my testimony because it was a significant turning point in my life, and it paved the way for me to become the person I am today. Trust me it has not been easy, and it will not be easy, but a positive thing can come out of a negative experience.

*"Whether you turn to the right or to the left, your ears will hear a voice behind you, saying, "This is the way, walk in it." - Isaiah 30:21*

Praise God and rejoice in the knowledge that he hears your prayers. Take life one day at a time, and thank God every step of the way. Let it comfort you to know that nothing can take away the close relationship you have with him. Your life is not the same and it is a choice you do not regret. I accept his decisions and course for my life. Though this has been one of the hardest things for me to do as a believer, because at times I do not agree or understand his ways. But, God is faithful, patient, loving, and full of grace. I could not ask for a better Father. My prayer is for you to experience and get to know God as I have.

VIRGINIA MARTIN

## POINTS FOR REFLECTION

*"Trust in the Lord with all your heart and lean not on your own understanding; in all your ways acknowledge him, and he will make your paths straight." – Proverbs 3:5-6*

Follow your intuition – if something or someone does not "feel" right, then it is best to step away from that person or thing. Once you accept Jesus Christ in your life, this is one of the ways the Holy Spirit talks to you. The Holy Spirit lives in me now, and I just have to listen carefully and let it guide me. This lets me make better choices. I may not like the answer or direction, but I have faith and believe God knows what is best for me.

Stay faithful to who you are – God made you to be unique. Do not lose your identity under any circumstances or let someone mold you to be someone else.

God does not give up on you – so neither should you. Lean on his strength to get you through. He can handle it.

I use to live with a lot of guilt, and beat myself up, especially when I made a bad decision. Don't do this to yourself, learn from your mistakes and grow from them. God forgives and loves you, so should you.

Gratitude – be grateful for every single thing you have, most importantly God, who is in your corner. I took for granted a lot of things before I became a believer. I learned to be humble and obedient from my experience. God is a teacher for life.

*"Humble yourself in the sight of the Lord, and He shall lift you up." – James 4:10*

Walk with God – I know this is not easy, sometimes you get pulled in a lot of directions. But, keep your focus on God and put him first. Do not let people, earthly influences and material possessions dictate the life you should live.

*"Your word is a lamp to my feet and a light for my path." – Psalm 119:105*

Look beyond the surface of any situation – the grass is not always greener on the other side. The enemy tries to make you think it is, but look closely at all the angles, take a step back, and pray on any decision you have to make. Be patient and wait on God's answer.

# 2 NO FEAR OF DARKNESS

*"I cried out to God for help; I cried out to God to hear me. When I was in distress, I sought the Lord; at night I stretched out untiring hands and my soul refused to be comforted." - Psalm 77:1-2*

As I child, I remember being sad, angry, withdrawn and lonely. I did not like to be alone or do things by myself. Perhaps because I was an only child, and had no siblings to talk or play with. I learned responsibility at a young age because my mother was sick a lot, and I had to help her in taking care of the house. In any event, I probably had symptoms of depression way back then, but did not think about it being a problem.

In my twenties and thirties, there were days I felt really down and could not explain why. One Friday I came home from work, went to my room and did not come out the whole weekend. I just lay in bed with no desire to do anything. I did not think to pray to God for help with the way I felt, and never thought to seek professional help either.

*"Though I have fallen, I will rise. Though I sit in darkness, the Lord will be my light." – Micah 7:8*

In 2011, I allowed certain relationships and situations get the best of me, and the depression I had learned to keep bottled down resurfaced. My emotions were on a rollercoaster ride, and I started spinning out of control. I knew something was really wrong when I did not want to get out of bed, sleep was my friend, my mind shut out the world, my body ached, and I felt lost, all alone, sad, and I did not care to care.

Even though I prayed and attended church, I felt the depression taking hold of me, and I felt too weak to fight it. I managed to go through the motions of living as if nothing was wrong, I smiled when I wanted to cry, and as far as anyone knew, I was all right. Yet, as much as the darkness consumed me, it became my best friend. I felt comfortable there. My world was falling to pieces, and I could no longer cope. I temporarily lost my faith in God, and felt he had abandoned me.

*"We must go through many hardships to enter the kingdom of God," they said.–Acts 14:22*

I went to see a psychotherapist and psychiatrist to try to figure out what was wrong with me. Talking to the psychotherapist helped to a certain point, and so did the anti-depressants I was prescribed, mostly they helped me lose weight. I tried to rise above it all, but I failed because I was counting on my own strength, and not God's, to get out of the pit I was in. My solution was to go quietly in the night, yet it was not an acceptable one in God's eyes. I felt the world would be better off without me, and I did not love myself enough to want to get out of the dark hole I was in.

*"I waited patiently for the Lord, He turned to me and heard my cry. He lifted me out of the slimy pit, out of the mud and mire; He set my feet on a rock and gave me a firm place to stand. He put a new song in my mouth, a hymn of praise to our God. Many will see and hear and put their trust in the Lord." – Psalm 40:1-3*

God, once again, became the light in my darkness, my strength in weakness. It was a slow process, but I did make it through, so I can tell you that you can too, just trust and believe in God, Jesus Christ and the Holy Spirit. Keep yourself above it all through prayer. I still struggle with depression, on occasion, but nowhere near what I used to. I am no longer afraid of being in a black hole because I have my faith to keep me out, and God's grace and love to shield me, even if it is from myself.

You are not alone, and you do not have to be ashamed, as I once was, that you are depressed or have depression. Find an outlet for those moments that you feel down, and do not let fear overwhelm you. My outlet is writing, others I know use art, just engage in something that gets you out of the mindset that pulls you to a sad place. My advice is to read the Bible, especially the Psalms and Proverbs. I find great comfort in these, and any other devotional, or inspiring book that boosts your self-confidence and self-esteem. Learn to only put positive thoughts in your head, and not let any situation control you, leave it in God's capable hands. Surround yourself with people that are in your corner, or join a support group. You do not have to fear darkness again. As hard as it may be at first, it is a matter of disciplining yourself to keep yourself up and know that God is there for and with you always.

I encourage you to hold on to God in the dark moments of your life, and let him be your light. In my case I know that it was God, Jesus Christ and the Holy Spirit that pulled me through and not the doctors, or pills. I never thought I would make it out. I thank God for his divine intervention in making things right. Step out in faith, and God will do the rest.

*"He heals the brokenhearted and binds up their wounds."*
*— Psalm 147:3*

# AFFIRMATIONS

Lord, give me strength to let go of my fear of darkness, so that it no longer has the power to paralyze me.

I am a daughter of God. He calls me friend. He stands by me in any circumstance. He has my back and won't ever forsake me. God's love for me is unconditional, no matter if I turn from him.

I embrace the darkness when it comes now, for it will not get the best of me. God is my light and he is in full control.

I follow God and I am not going to fall again in the dark hole I was in, no matter what is going on in my life. God has equipped me for battle and is by my side, leading me to victory.

# POINTS FOR REFLECTION

*"For you did not receive a spirit that makes you a slave again to fear, but you received the Spirit of sonship."*

*– Romans 8:15*

The enemy attacks where you are most weak. Pray to God to make you strong and not let the weak areas in your life be a foothold for the enemy.

You only stay in a black hole if you don't reach out for God's hand to keep you out.

No one is better than God to light the way out of darkness.

You are worthy, God has a purpose for you, hold on to that.

# 3 HIS TIMING

*"Be still before the Lord and wait patiently for him..."*
*Psalm 37:7*

In the New International Version of the Bible, the definition of Patience is "able to put up with problems or pain without complaining or becoming angry". I thought it was more like not waiting before doing something or acting impulsively without giving any thought to what you did. I can apply, both the Bible definition and my perception of patience, to my life at one point or another.

Patience has been one of the hardest things for me to learn, understand and practice. I wanted God to answer my prayer(s) as soon as I asked for something, and it took me a while to fully comprehend that this was not the way it worked. God does not "hop" to your request, and you must wait on his response and accept his denial or delay in getting you what you asked for.

On September 1, 2012, I wrote on a wall calendar these words: "My mission begins". It was the start of me living a Christ-like life. Even though I had received Jesus Christ as my Lord and Savior a few years before, I still felt that I had to openly commit to God and start my walk with him.

I prayed for strength to deal with what life threw at me, patience to understand God's will for me, faith to know it would not last forever, and hope that there were better days ahead. I believe growing in faith has a lot to do with being patient and waiting on God's timing. I knew that I had to go through many trials and tests, develop my endurance to withstand the challenges of everyday life and place total trust in God.

At times I wanted to walk with God at a pace faster than what he had in mind. He would pull back the reigns to teach me that he was in control at all times. It has taken me years to learn that God sees beyond the here and now, and that when something does not go my way and I get something different, or not at all, there is a reason for it. God does know best.

*"But the fruit of the Spirit is love, joy, peace, patience, kindness, goodness, faithfulness, gentleness and self-control." - Galatians 5:22-23*

In one of the church services I attended, the pastor talked about Patience. I took notes and want to share them with you here:

Be patient and do not give up. Patient prayers allow you to see God and yourself more clearly. Faith says that you are going to believe and trust God and Jesus Christ.

God delays to give us what we want because he cares for us. His delays are for our good even if the reasons are hidden from us. When we give God access he will bring assurance to us. There is a process in God's delays. God may not come when you want him to, but he is always on time. God's timing is not our timing, we must trust in him. Have small and big conversations with God. God brings the power, he wants you to bring the patience.

*"Be joyful always, pray continually; give thanks in all circumstances, for this is God's will for you in Christ Jesus." – 1 Thessalonians 4:18*

Have an active, patient, prayer life with God and practice patience. Wait patiently on the Lord and have hope in his words. We must be patient in our prayer because of our connection to the True Vine. Jesus is our only source of strength. God's delays are not God's denials because he does not respond on our time. His delay is just saying "be patient."

*"And we urge you, brothers, warn those who are idle, encourage the timid, help the weak, be patient with everyone." – 1 Thessalonians 4:14*

# POINTS FOR REFLECTION

God knows what time it is, and does not need to be reminded. Your urgency is not his urgency. Wait on his timing in your life.

Control the parts of your life that you can, and leave the rest to God.

Be patient on the things you pray for. God sees all and does his best to steer you in the right direction. Wait on his answer, he will make it known what it is.

If you really think about it, it makes sense to wait on God. Do not rush into making a wrong choice or decide on something in the spur of the moment. It is better to be patient and wait, than to be impulsive and then have to deal with regret and adverse consequences.

Your prayer does not fall on deaf ears. God listens attentively to your prayers. Though your prayers may seem to go unanswered, have patience, he is working on your request, but only if it aligns with his will for you.

*"But when you pray, go into your room, close the door and pray to your Father, who is unseen. Then your Father, who sees what is done in secret, will reward you." -*

*Matthew 6:6*

Patience means letting go and understanding that God is in control.

*"Do not be anxious about anything, but in everything, by prayer and petition, with thanksgiving, present your requests to God. And the peace of God, which transcends all understanding, will guard your hearts and minds in Christ Jesus." – Philippians 4:6-7*

Everything has a time and place. Accepting life as it comes, and trusting God, is a true practice in patience.

*"The Lord is not slow in keeping his promise, as some understand slowness. Instead he is patient with you, not wanting anyone to perish, but everyone to come to repentance." - 2 Peter 3:9*

# 4 HOPE

*"But hope that is seen is no hope at all. Who hopes for what he already has? But if we hope for what we do not yet have, we wait for it patiently." - Romans 8:24-25*

There is a simple plan to holding on to hope. You have to believe that hope pulls you out of a certain situation, gives you something to look forward to and gives you the boost you need to not only exist and survive, but also to live. I believe and trust that God is a powerful being who, even if I stumble, he is there to lend a hand. There is no need to be afraid of the life that we are led to live. God provides us strength and uses our brokenness to bless us in unexpected ways. God rescued me from drowning in the sea of darkness, by throwing me the life jacket I needed to swim to shore. My hope has been restored many times over.

*"He gives strength to the weary and increases the power of*

*the weak.  Even youths grow tired and weary, and young men stumble and fall; but those who hope in the LORD will renew their strength.  They will soar on wings like eagles; they will run and not grow weary, they will walk and not be faint." - Isaiah 40:29-31*

## MY PRAYER FOR YOU

God, please help my brothers and sisters know your righteousness and promises.  Teach them to understand what a mighty God you are.  Let them cast their burdens on you and leave them there.  Free up their souls to worship you and minister to others.  Make their hearts strong and not lose hope and faith in you. Through every circumstance have them keep the focus on you.  Lord, please meet them in all the areas that they need you.  Amen.

You are part of God's sheep, he is the Good Shepherd. Even if you get separated from the flock, it is not acceptable to God.  He loves you and watches over you. When you are lost, you need God to give you direction and set you on the right path.  He gives you the hope you need to carry on.  Discipline yourself to hear his voice and obey his will for you.

What has God shown you? Think back to situations in your life that God has been there, with a rope, life jacket, another person, prayer, or church, to get you out and give you hope.  You may not have realized it at the time, but it was all coming from him. This is the God to love and serve.

*For I am convinced that neither death nor life, neither angels nor demons, neither the present nor the future, nor any powers, neither height nor depth, nor anything else in all creation, will be able to separate us from the love of God that is in Christ Jesus our Lord. – Romans 8:33-39*

There cannot be a stronger bible verse than the one above. It assures you that you are attached to God through Jesus Christ, and it is an unbreakable bond. Hope is the light that flickers and burns eternally when you remain steadfast with faith.

What is hope? Here are a few examples of what hope is to me:

God in my heart, soul, mind and spirit

Each day that I breathe, for I have life

A light in darkness

A heartfelt prayer

A happy memory

A garden full of my favorite flowers

A shoulder to cry on

Comforting words from a friend

Someone who understands and believes in me

A soul mate that withstands the test of time and space

An inspirational book

Having joy and  peace within me

Understanding that "This too shall pass"

A loving hug

Anything that makes me come alive

Knowing that I have a place in Heaven

Hope is faith on fire

# POINTS FOR REFLECTION

The eternal hope in us:

*"And we know that in all things God works for the good of those who love him, who have been called according to his purpose." - Romans 8:28*

H.O.P.E.

Having Optimistic Persistent Encouragement

Always have HOPE – No matter how grim and desperate the situation.

# GOD WILL DO FOR YOU - POEM

God will do for you.

The skies may not always be blue, no sun but mist and fog. But in your heart may you know that God will do for you. When the days are gloomy, with just storm after storm, be patient in prayer and hopeful that God will do for you.

Where the road is never ending, and every door seems to be closing, stay strong and praise the Lord.

God will do for you.

# 5 THE MUSTARD SEED

*"I tell you the truth, if you have faith as small as a mustard seed, you can say to this mountain, 'Move from here to there' and it will move. Nothing will be impossible for you." – Matthew 17:20*

Be an ambassador for God by planting a seed in others (through words, actions or prayers) to glorify him. The seed planted in me by another believer several years ago, led me to seek a deeper understanding of God, and the importance of having him in my life. I attend a local Christian church, read the Bible, pray every day, and do my best to live a peaceful life. Therefore, it is now my turn to pay it forward, and share my testimony, so that others may thirst for God and His word.

*"Therefore go and make disciples of all nations, baptizing them in the name of the Father and of the Son and of the Holy Spirit and teaching them to obey everything I have commanded you. And surely I am with you always, to the very end of the age." - Matthew 28:19-20*

Before I could start "planting", I had to first forgive those that had hurt me. I did this in silent prayer, freeing myself from the feelings of bitterness, betrayal and regret. I exposed my soul and opened up to God to make me whole again. I realized that in order to show God my love for him, I had to love as he loves. I can't live my life without the strength God gives me each day. I pray to not miss an opportunity to minister to someone and let them know that he is alive and well. He is here to bless, teach, redeem, forgive, and protect you, so that he can build a relationship with you, as his most prized possession.

*"Therefore, get rid of all moral filth and the evil that is so prevalent and humbly accept the word planted in you, which can save you." – James 1:21*

You are not meant to save anyone just because you plant a seed, which is God's word. God is the one that rescues and saves, not you. Do not take that responsibility and limit those you can touch by burdening yourself with it. Be bold and go into the world and share your smile, love, a kind word, kindness, warm hug, attentive ear, and know you are doing your part to glorify God's name. All you need is a willing and obedient heart and he takes care of all the rest.

*"What shall we say the kingdom of God is like, or what parable shall we use to describe it? It is like a mustard seed, which is the smallest seed you plant in the ground. Yet when planted, it grows and becomes the largest of all garden plants, with such big branches that the birds of the air can perch in its shade." – Mark 4:30-32*

You grow God's kingdom by ministering to people you may encounter in your everyday life. This does not mean that you need to approach people. It can be someone at work who is going through trials, and just needs someone to listen to them. You can take the opportunity to offer comforting words, especially if you have been through a similar situation. It is all about making a connection in some way so that the other person "sees" your faith and belief in God, by your actions and behavior.

Even if you do not know Scripture, you can point others to the Bible as a source of inspiration, or to your church for a sense of community. Think of the time you accepted Jesus Christ as your Lord and Savior, and ways in which this changed your life, and way of thinking. What transformation took place within you? This is the testimony you share with others in order to plant that "mustard seed" in them. The hope is that the person turns around and does the same thing to someone else, and so on and so on. We build on each other for the glory of God.

I love my job because I interact with many people and I get the opportunity to help those that I see in need of an encouraging word, or even a hug. People share their stories sometimes of their difficulties, and I do my best to uplift their spirit. I pray to God to give me the right words to say to offer comfort. I try to be obedient in whatever God calls me to do. You can do this, just believe in the Holy Spirit within you. God looks forward to reaping the plentiful harvest that you helped to sow.

*"But the one who received the seed that fell on good soil is the man who hears the word and understands it. He produces a crop, yielding a hundred, sixty or thirty times what was sown." - Matthew 12:23*

## POINTS FOR REFLECTION

*"Come, follow me, Jesus said, "and I will send you out to fish for people." – Matthew 4:19*

Faith grows from a planted seed in you and then your true relationship with God begins.

*"For we are God's workmanship, created in Christ Jesus to do good works, which God prepared in advance for us to do."- Ephesians 2:10*

All you can do is your part to the best of your God given ability, to plant a "mustard seed" wherever God gives you the opportunity to do so. Share your testimony with others of his grace in your life.

*"No one who does a miracle in my name can in the next moment say anything bad about me, for whoever is not against us is for us. I tell you the truth, anyone who gives you a cup of water in my name because you belong to Christ will certainly not lose his reward." – Mark 9:39-41*

# 6 GOD, MY FATHER

*"Know then in your heart that as a man disciplines his son,*
*so the LORD, your God disciplines you."*

*– Deuteronomy 8:5*

I believe some people stay away from God because they do not have a true notion of who he really is. I grew up having a perception of God as someone in the heavens, far away from me, and unreachable, even by prayer. Therefore, my prayers at that time were made with little or no conviction, because I thought he was not really "listening" anyway. For a long time I believed that God did not love me, and that every wrong or bad thing that happened in my life was punishment from him. I did not understand, and no one ever really explained, that God was also my Father, just one in the spiritual sense. He was a stranger to me, and so was Jesus Christ. I knew the story about Jesus, yet had no connection or relationship with him, and only attended church because my mother forced me to. I did not get the picture that God was and is a loving Father.

God teaches you through life lessons, he withholds things from you that are not good, or gives it to you after a while when he feels the time is right. However, he does not make it easy, because he is preparing you to live this earthly life that has so many twists and turns. God does not sugarcoat anything, he is real with you by being faithful, caring, protective, and nurturing. He teaches you and helps you develop as a Christian and grow in faith and relationship with him, through your experiences in the highs and lows of life. Is this so different than what an earthly father does? God does not give in to your tantrums when things do not go your way, and he is not one you should put to the test. You don't always get what you want, but you do get what you need.

*"Obviously, I'm not trying to win the approval of people, but of GOD. If pleasing people were my goal, I would not be Christ's servant." –Galatians 1:10 (NLT)*

God takes care of your needs, not wants, in order that you can survive and really live this life. He showers you with love and grace through the Holy Spirit and forgives your sins through Jesus Christ. He lives in the believer's spirit and is not going anywhere. You are his child forever, and he is your role model. Once you see God in this way, everything he does through other people, and circumstances makes sense and allows for you to have a close, long lasting relationship with him. Let him in your life!

*"The Lord is the strength of my life" –Psalm 27:1*

Blessed are you who have an earthly father as well as a heavenly one. I praise the Lord, he takes away with lessons, yet rewards with blessings. Though you may falter, and lose sight of God, always find your way back to him. You experience your time on Earth in a totally different way.

*"Therefore, as we have opportunity, let us do good to all people, especially to those who belong to the family of believers."- Galatians 6:10 (NIV)*

This is the God I know: *"The salvation of the righteous comes from the Lord; He is their stronghold in time of trouble. The Lord helps them and delivers them; he delivers them from the wicked and saves them because they took refuge in him". – Psalm 37:39-40*

# GOD IS STILL STANDING – A POEM

*"If you do not stand firm in your faith, you will not stand at all."- Isaiah 7:9*

God is still standing. Don't forsake or mock him.
He is a timeless treasure, which no one can measure.
Our sins are forgiven and we are redeemed, for he is our Savior above all things.
God works in mysterious ways.
We must be patient and not be dismayed.
Relief is to come soon enough, even though each day continues to be tough.
Pray to him with all your might.
Always know wrong from right.
I am on my knees now, it has been too long since my faith made me strong.
Loneliness will be no more.
My head is held high as I walk through the door.

# AFFIRMATION

*"I do not hide your righteousness in my heart; I speak of your faithfulness and salvation." – Psalm 40:10*

God you are the strength in my weakness. You help me carry on when my spirit is down, and hope is lost. Please help me to always see the bigger picture and to recognize current circumstances as the temporary situations that they are. All I do is for your glory, not mine. Through your words and wisdom, I want to offer others a door to open themselves up to you and your amazing grace. Lord, I am nothing without you. Thank you for showing up, and staying steadfast by my side.

VIRGINIA MARTIN

# POINTS FOR REFLECTION

*"But as for me, it is good to be near God. I have made the Sovereign LORD my refuge; I will tell of all your deeds."*
*– Psalm 73:28*

God does not leave me alone in my storms, but stands beside me holding an umbrella.

When you feel off track, out of focus, lost, and confused, pray to God for support and strength.

Read Psalm 34 so you can know what God, the Father, does for those who believe and have faith in him.

# 7 STEP OUT IN FAITH

*"If the Lord delights in a man's way, he makes his steps firm; though he stumble, he will not fall, for the Lord upholds him with his hand." – Psalm 37:23-24*

What does it mean to "Step Out In Faith"? I struggled with this concept, but have finally understood its significance, and it is life changing. It has given me a whole new perspective on faith and what it does in, to and through me. I have learned to relinquish control and let God do the worrying for me, take the path he guides me to, and let him do the rest. I can trust that I can fall back with no net, and that he is there to catch me.

*"Put on the full armor of God so that you can take your stand against the devil's schemes." – Ephesians 6:11*

I encourage you to "step out in faith" so that you too can experience the peace it brings you and the burdens it lifts off your shoulders. It is a work in progress, but do not give up, you will get to that point, as I have, in spite of your struggles and affliction. After I accepted Jesus Christ in my life, the enemy, in its various forms, started to attack me in full force, testing my faith to its limits. Many times I faltered and cried out to God for mercy and relief from it all. However, with my suffering came growing faith, which made me stronger, to the point that, even if I do not like to go through trials, I know that a blessing is waiting for me on the other side of it. The less I fear the bad things that happen, the more I overcome the enemy's attacks in my areas of weakness. This is another way to step out in faith.

*"Give your worries to the Lord, and he will take care of you. He will never let good people down."*

*- Psalm 55:22 (NCV)*

There was a time that I had a disconnect, big time, with my younger daughter. We were at each other throats, and spoke harsh words to each other. As much as I tried to make her see the error of her ways, and adjust mine, nothing was happening, and our relationship kept snow balling into a black hole. I knew I had done all I could as a parent, and I could not keep blaming myself for her actions and behavior. It was then that in prayer, I gave her up to God. I asked that he take care of her, and make her see the light and give her a new sense of direction. I should have done this long before, because it was so liberating to release the struggle I had with my daughter go into God's powerful hands. Having faith in him to take care of her and mend our relationship gave me peace. I finally let God, her Father in Heaven, take the reign and deal with her, as only he could. Today, I am happy to say that she has God front and center in her life. The Holy Spirit lives within her and her faith guides every step that she takes.

*"Consider it pure joy, my brother, whenever you face trials of many kinds, because you know that the testing of your faith develops perseverance. Perseverance must finish its work so that you may be mature and complete, not lacking anything." - James 1:2-6*

God restores you so that you can help others, with your testimony, be restored and renewed. Do not let an opportunity pass you by in which you can serve God in this manner. You show him your love by loving others, and sharing with them what he has done for you.

Know and feel in your heart, spirit, mind, and soul that you are unique, made in God's image, and therefore very special. You enhance the world and others' lives by being in it. You touch lives without even knowing it. You are not a mistake and you are not in this world by accident. No matter how alone, afraid, desperate, angry, frustrated you may feel, keep God close to you at all times. He protects and guide you every step of the way. Thank God for your blessings, to him be the glory. Keep in mind that things are not always what they seem, but your faith will set you free. Opportunity awaits in the most unexpected places. Be open to that. I truly believe that through bad, good things come, but it just might take a while to get it. Learn to get out of your comfort zone, this allows you to grow, and try your best to face what you most fear, this is where courage comes in. Even though it is hard to rise above your circumstances when it is staring you in the face and you are in the thick of it, God is constant through it all, and stands firm, so step out in faith.

*"Blessed is the man who perseveres under trial, because when he has stood the test, he will receive the crown of life that God has promised to those who love him."*

*– James 1:12*

# AFFIRMATION

*"Do you not know that in a race all runners run, but only one gets the prize? Run in such a way as to get the prize."*
*– 1 Corinthians 9:24*

God, I cannot thank you enough. Even when I am angry estranged, and rebuke you, you stand by my side. Many are the times you carry me through trials. There is no greater Father than you. Please continue to nurture my soul with your grace. May I find the right words to say, even on my bad days and let others know how worthy you are of praise. Let me step out in faith so that I may know the peace and joy that doing so brings. I want just enough to fully live this life abundantly and be ready to meet you when my day comes.

# A PRAYER FOR TIMES OF AFFLICTION

There is a force at hand, the enemy wants to pull me in. God, help me fight, don't let that evil spirit win. What big plans must you have for me? That I am being tested so much and my soul is being pushed to the dark side without control. But, I am pushing back, God. Asking for your help and strength. Shield me, Oh Lord, and cover me with your cloak. I am your child wanting to do good, anointed I may be. Is this why there is such an attack on me? Lord, I lift up my hands to you, not much else for me to do. You are my Savior and Redeemer. Bless me and give me what you have promised me. Lift up my spirit, God, so that my faith in you can set me free. Amen.

# POINTS FOR REFLECTION

Do not give up your faith, or hope in your salvation through Jesus Christ.

Pray this bible verse to grow and keep you strong in faith: *"Make me know your ways, O Lord; Teach me your paths. Lead me in your truth and teach me, for you are the God of my salvation; for you I wait all day."- Psalm 25:4-5*

Let your saving grace be prayer, always, for whatever bad situation you are going through. Leave it in God's hands and do not take it back. That is all you have to do.

Practice selflessness in order to fully relinquish your will to God.

Give God the credit he deserves, glorify his name to others by stepping out in faith.

VIRGINIA MARTIN

# 8 SPIRITUAL REINFORCEMENT

*"The Sovereign LORD has given me an instructed tongue, to know the word that sustains the weary. He wakens me morning by morning, wakens my ear to listen like one being taught." – Isaiah 50:4*

What inspires, motivates and uplifts your spirit? In those times that I am most challenged by difficult situations, or I run out of steam, I find comfort in reading the Psalms, Proverbs, and other inspiring Scripture. Also, I write my favorite ones in a journal so that I can read them whenever I need encouragement, and a "boost" of spiritual refreshment.

Attending church and listening to God's word and message is another source of spiritual reinforcement. It is important that you seek God always, but especially in those moments when you need his strength to get you through a trial that tests your faith. Awaken your mind, heart, soul and spirit by meditating and reflecting in the ways God can move you forward in your own spiritual journey. In this chapter, I share some Scripture readings, inspirational quotes and thoughts that have touched me and given me guidance to follow the path God sets before me.

## BIBLE VERSES TO NOURISH YOUR SOUL

"Though I walk in the midst of trouble, you preserve my life; you stretch out your hand against the anger of my foes." Psalm 138:7

"Let him who walks in the dark, who has no light, trust in the name of the LORD and rely on his God." – Isaiah 50:10

"Every good and perfect gift is from above, coming down from the Father of the heavenly lights, who does not change like shifting shadows." – James 1:17

"When I said, "My foot is slipping," your love, O Lord, supported me. When anxiety was great within me, your consolation brought joy to my soul." — Psalm 94:18-19

"He will cover you with his feathers, and under his wings you will find refuge; his faithfulness will be your shield and rampart." – Psalm 91:4

"And I am sure that God, who began the good work within you, will continue his work until it is finally finished on that day when Christ Jesus comes back again." Philippians 1:6 (NLT)

"Therefore do not worry about tomorrow for tomorrow will worry about itself. Each day has enough trouble of its own." – Matthew 6:34

"Praise be to the God and Father of our Lord Jesus Christ, the Father of compassion and the God of all comfort, who comforts us in all our troubles, so that we can comfort those in any trouble with the comfort we ourselves have received from God." – 2 Corinthians 1:3-4

"Don't worry about anything; instead, pray about everything. Tell God what you need, and thank him for all he has done – Philippians 5:6 (NLT)

"I have told you these things, so that in me you may have peace. In this world you will have trouble. But take heart! I have overcome the world." – John 16:33

# Inspirational quotes to keep you close to God

Prayer connects the dots to God.

Do not be idle in worshipping God. Glorify and praise him for his works and never ending grace.

Get on your knees and pray. Tomorrow is a brand new day, to restore your soul and forget it all.

Don't let go of hope. The Hope Line is faith in God, prayer, reading the Bible, fellow believers in Christ, and the Church.

Let go of the past. There is no need to go down a road that leads you to walk around in circles, and does not propel you forward.

I am comforted in my sorrow, for God takes care of the brokenhearted.

Guide me, Lord, and lead my life in the way that gives you glory.

God give me peace in my slumber, strength in my spirit and faith in my walk.

Anything worthwhile is worth the effort to get it, and the faith to maintain it.

Establish and maintain relationships that support you in your spiritual journey, and walk with God.

With inner peace I have everything. It is where my clear thoughts flow and the light shines.

True wealth is the knowledge of God and his limitless resources. Be thankful every day for everything.

Sometimes you have to get out of your own way, and stop being your own worst enemy. God loves you, remember that.

Take each day as a blessing, even when it does not seem like one.

# POINTS FOR REFLECTION TO EXPERIENCE GOD'S GRACE

If you accept this life as just passing through, do not anchor yourself to material things. By so doing, you experience a freer life, in which you can move to God's calling.

Life is a series of tests. Some you pass, fail or get an incomplete. God will repeat the test for every lesson he wants to teach you, and you have not yet learned.

Let God have an open door in your life. Do not limit his access. Once you let him be in control, you can bounce back from what life throws at you.

In the process of healing you reinvent yourself. It is not easy, for you have to fill old hurts with new hope, and each renewal shapes the person you are meant to be.

You have hidden talents inside of you. Take time to dig them out, and polish them. Be confident in the abilities God gave you.

Before you start your day, spend quiet time in prayer and reflection. Be united with God.

Forgive those that have hurt you, release any anger against them to God. He rewards your suffering and his grace heals you. Once you have joy in your heart, it cannot be taken away. Your spirit is free, open to love, and new possibilities.

Your job as a believer is never done. Whether good or bad, any lesson learned is an opportunity for growth and hidden blessings. Praise God and press forward in your faith. Pass it on to others to glorify his name.

Life's challenges, trials and tribulations are just a temporary fork in the road. You are only human and your faith will wander, but God makes sure it does not wander far. He did not get you this far to let you go.

Action words to apply to your life: *Encourage, Inspire, Reflect, Believe, Hope, Faith, Endurance, Enlightenment, Commitment, Dedication, Focus, Motivation, Determination, Strength, Courage, Love.*

# 9 JUST ENOUGH

*"When we operate from a place of humility, he gives us more grace."—James 4:6*

You may think you need more friends, money, toys for your children, cars, trips, clothes, shoes, food, the latest in technology, but you don't. All this "stuff" blocks your ability to hear God clearly because it occupies your mind with "clutter". God provides just enough of what you need to live and exist.

Wake up, look around you, and do not be so caught up in the hustle and bustle of life that you miss out on the true beauty of living. God created so many beautiful things for you to enjoy, and you may not even notice them because of your busy schedule. Don't "over pack" your days with things to do and places to go. Leave yourself down time each day to pray, recharge, reflect and renew your mind, body and soul. Doing this is part of living with just enough, and becoming a minimalist to learn to do more with less. It also means simplifying your life style, and making time to do what is important and meaningful.

I used to be a person that was not happy unless I worried about something, and projected a "what if" scenario of the future. I did not let things go and wanted to control my world as much as possible. I was not present in the moment enjoying and appreciating the people and things that God gave me. Through the "school of hard knocks" I learned that he is enough and the only one in control. All I have to do is give my worries over to him, so that I can have peace of mind.

Not being happy with "just enough" also cost me a lot of unhappiness and financial hardships. I overcharged my credit cards buying unnecessary stuff, and lived beyond my means. At one point, I was totally broke, looking at eviction because I did not have all the money to pay the rent. God had mercy on me, because I received $500 from my aunt who had no knowledge of the hardship I was going through. This was just enough to complete the money I owed for rent. God has pulled through for me many times when money was tight. I am blessed to have him in my life and am forever thankful for everything he has done for me.

Through my "just enough' moments I learned humility and "died to self". It is no longer about me, it is all about

God, because he needs to be the focus of everything I do. I am happier now than I have ever been before, because I have a close relationship with him, Jesus Christ and the Holy Spirit to keep me on track. I give back to God by donating more money at church, being a volunteer, and loving people more. I feel I am finally doing God's work and it feels so good to know that.

Just enough means just that. I live within my means now, though I am still paying the consequences of not managing my money well. God has advised me on ways to cut down on my expenses, and I am trying to eliminate, or donate things I do not need. I do not overwhelm myself with petty nonsense or waste unnecessary time, yet I can truly appreciate and value my job, home, friends, and family. I have enough furniture, clothes, food, money to pay bills, and on occasion extra money to go out to dinner, the movies, or on vacation. God has enriched my life by supplying all that I need, and sometimes allowing me to get what I want.

*"...for I have learned to be content whatever the circumstances. I know what it is to be in need, and I know what it is to have plenty; I have learned the secret of being content in any and every situation, whether well fed or hungry, whether living in plenty or in want, I can do everything through him who gives me strength." –*
*Philippians 4:11-13*

VIRGINIA MARTIN

# POINTS FOR REFLECTION

*"Do nothing out of selfish ambition or vain conceit. Rather, in humility value others above yourselves, not looking to your own interests but each of you to the interests of the others." – Philippians 2:3-4*

In order to fully love God and others you have to "die to self", yet still love yourself.

Detach yourself from material things. Free your spirit with God's word, worship him and glorify his name by making your life about what he wills for you to do, and accept what he wills for your life.

Be joyful, Keep praying, Be thankful.

God always finds a way to bless us with what we need and that is just enough.

Though he may not always answer, God always listens. Your best listening to him happens in silence.

You know when you do wrong. You need to ask God for forgiveness, so you can get back on track and in favor with him.

Free your mind of unnecessary distractions, and leave room for God's word to seep in. Enjoy the little things, and practice minimalist living. This helps you feel light, unburdened, and spiritually charged.

You have to discipline yourself with just enough, it is not easy, but it can be done.

Living abundantly does not mean having more things. God wants you to have what you desire, as long as it aligns with what he knows you need. This touches all areas of your life: love, family, friends, work, and other relationships.

It is the simple and little things that really matter, and give the most joy and satisfaction in life.

*"And the Lord shall guide thee continually, and satisfy your soul in drought." - Isaiah 58:11*

# 10 FAITH WITHOUT BORDERS

*"And without faith it is impossible to please God, because anyone who comes to him must believe that he exists and that he rewards those who earnestly seek him."*

*- Hebrews 11:6*

Faith without borders is unconditional and limitless. It is faith that you do not pick and choose as you will, based on your circumstances. Faith is the key element in believing that God exists, you cannot establish a relationship with God without it. However, it has taken me years to "let go, and let God", and by so doing show him my trust in his power to make all things right. When you can do nothing about a situation, and all you have left is prayer, faith provides the hope that "this too shall pass".

My faith has been tested many times since I fully accepted God and Jesus Christ into my life. The enemy has tried to knock me down at every opportunity, using my areas of weakness to create doubt about my abilities and shake my faith in God. At times he has succeeded, if only for a moment, to get me away from the God I serve. But, prayer and reading the Bible have been a source of comfort that not all is lost, and I have been pulled back into God's grace.

Talking faithfully to God, asking for his help and direction, alleviated the burdens I carried. He gave me the rope I needed to pull out. I have learned through my trials that the key is to keep the focus on God at all times, keep faith strong and not lose hope.

*"We live by faith, not by sight." - 2 Corinthians 5:7*

There is something on the other side of suffering. You do not see it, for it is hidden until the time is right for it to come out. But when the blessing comes, you understand the "why" of the things you go through. I think the biggest challenge for a believer is to trust that your pain is not in vain. Your faith grows in hardships because you depend on God to give you the strength and endurance you need to persevere. Faith causes growing pains, yet with each growth spurt comes maturity to understand God's ways.

*"As a prisoner for the Lord, then, I urge you to live a life worthy of the call you have received"- Ephesians 4:1-6*

Even at your wit's end, God is there to lend a hand. I am not saying it is easy, because it is not. But, God has proven to me, time and again, that good things do come in the most unexpected places, ways, and times. As you go through each and every trial, this becomes more apparent to you. You need to put on God's shield and arm yourself with the Holy Spirit. God walks in your steps each and every time. He leads at times when you have lost your way or he lets you find it on your own, though he is never far behind. God carries you when you can no longer walk or have any strength to go on. Give it all to him, he is in control of your life, especially in your moments of despair. Show your faith to others by being Christ-like in the way you live your life. I am a witness that you can see light past the darkness, overcome your obstacles, and move forward. All it takes is faith.

*"But he said to me, 'My grace is sufficient for you, for my power is made perfect in weakness.' Therefore I will boast all the more gladly about my weaknesses, so that Christ's power may rest on me. That is why for Christ's sake, I delight in weaknesses, in insults, in hardships, in persecutions, in difficulties. For when I am weak, then I am strong." - 2 Corinthians 12:9-10*

VIRGINIA MARTIN

.

# POEM: FREEING THE SELF

Freeing the self to be bold. To tell the stories untold. Face fears of old, and be free from the chains of the past.

Exposing who you are. It is not easy and the road is long. But the world is full of flowers and the birds full of song. Start one day at a time.

There is pain and tears through the years. What you did or could have done. The love you had or left behind.

To truly and fully know yourself is one of the hardest things to do. It leaves you exposed and nowhere to go.

But, I have embarked on this spiritual journey of self discovery. There are bumpy roads ahead I know, as I dig deeper into my soul.

My mother raised me right. I have not let her down. She can be proud of who I am and that I have always done what I can.

Finally, I am one with myself, keeping faith and hope alive. I have an internal peace I had not experienced before, all because I let God in the door.

# POINTS FOR REFLECTION

*"In the same way, faith by itself, if it is not accompanied by action, is dead." "You see that his faith and his actions were working together, and his faith was made complete by what he did." - James 2:17, 22*

### FAITH is:

Knowing that whatever God brings you to, he will bring you through.

Trusting that God is always with you. Even when you don't "hear" or "feel" him, and your prayers seem to go unanswered.

Keeping hope alive, even when circumstances are impossible or overwhelming.

Having limitless faith in all things, all the time.

Loving God unconditionally, and above all things.

Praying with true conviction and trusting God to know what is best for you, even if you do not see what that is.

Being obedient to God's will.

Reading God's word to build an intimate relationship with him.

Faith helps you cope when nothing in your life makes sense.

Having a reining ear to hear God's voice.

Believing that God loves you no matter what, and meets you where you are.

God gives you grace, and expects back faith.

Faith is being attacked from all directions, and looking up to God in prayer.

# FOR FURTHER READING

*The Bible* – any version

*Scripture readings*:

Psalm 13

Psalm 18:28, 30-36

Psalm 30:10-12

Psalm 46:10

Psalm 51:10-12

Psalm 61:1-4

Psalm 62:5-8

Psalm 67

Psalm 119:153-160

Psalm 126:5

Proverbs 4:10-12

James 1:2-8, 12, 22-25

2 Timothy 4:7

Galatians 6:9

Ephesians 4:1-13

Isaiah 26:4

Luke 8:11-15

Romans 8:18-21, 28-39

Romans 12

Philippians 3:14, 4:9

Jeremiah 10:23

Job 19:25

1 Corinthians 16:13-14

1 John 1:5-7

John 14:26-27

Hebrews 11

1 Chronicles 28:9

*God's Promises*® - for every day– New Century Version, by Word Publishing, 1996

*Streams in the Desert*, by L.B. Cowman – edited by Jim Reimann

*A Year With C.S. Lewis*, by C. S. Lewis - edited by Patricia S. Klein

*The Miracles In You*, by Mark Victor Hansen

*How to Hear from God*, by Joyce Meyer

*Wisdom for Everyday Living*, by Steve M. Woods

*Hope for Every Moment*, by T. D. Jakes

# ABOUT THE AUTHOR

Virginia Martin has a Bachelor's degree in Business Administration from Florida Atlantic University. She lives in South Florida, but grew up in New York City. Virginia has worked over 18 years as a Human Resources Professional, the past 15 years in the healthcare industry.

Virginia has been passionate about writing from a young age, and debuts as an author with the devotional, *Faith Without Borders.* She is a member of the Florida Writers Association, Romance Writers of America and Florida Romance Writers. Virginia loves books, and dreams of owning a bookshop one day. She enjoys reading the Bible, poetry, devotionals, mystery/suspense and romance. Her next works in progress are an inspirational poetry book and romance novella.

To contact Virginia Martin, or to be placed on a mailing list to receive updates about new releases, click the "*Contact Me*" page on her author blog: www.virginiamartinauthor.net.

Be part of the *Faith Without Borders* Fan Club:

Send a picture of you, with this book, to virginiamartinauthor@gmail.com.

# Thank you for supporting this book.

If you enjoyed it, please consider sharing it with others by:

- Talking about it in a Facebook post, tweeting about it, pinning it on Pinterest, uploading a picture via Instagram or writing a blog post.

- Word of mouth recommendation to your circle of family and friends, book club, and workplace.

- "LIKE" my Facebook page: facebook.com/mywritingself, and post a comment as to what you liked best about the book.

- Buy it for someone you know who would benefit from its message.

- Write a book review on Amazon, Goodreads, Barnes and Noble, your website or blog.

50198279R00057

Made in the USA
Charleston, SC
17 December 2015